FRANCE

Written by Doug Barone

PowerKiDS
press

Published in 2025
by The Rosen Publishing Group, Inc.
2544 Clinton Street, Buffalo, NY 14224

© 2024 BookLife Publishing Ltd.

Written by: Doug Barone
Edited by: Elise Carraway
Designed by: Ker Ker Lee

Cataloging-in-Publication Data

Names: Barone, Doug.
Title: France / Doug Barone.
Description: Buffalo, NY : PowerKids Press, 2025. | Series: Countries of the world | Includes glossary and index.
Identifiers: ISBN 9781499449198 (pbk.) | ISBN 9781499449204 (library bound) | ISBN 9781499449211 (ebook)
Subjects: LCSH: France--Juvenile literature.
Classification: LCC DC17.B376 2025 | DDC 944--dc23

Manufactured in the United States of America

CPSIA Compliance Information: Batch #CW25PK. For further information contact Rosen Publishing at 1-800-237-9932.

Find us on  

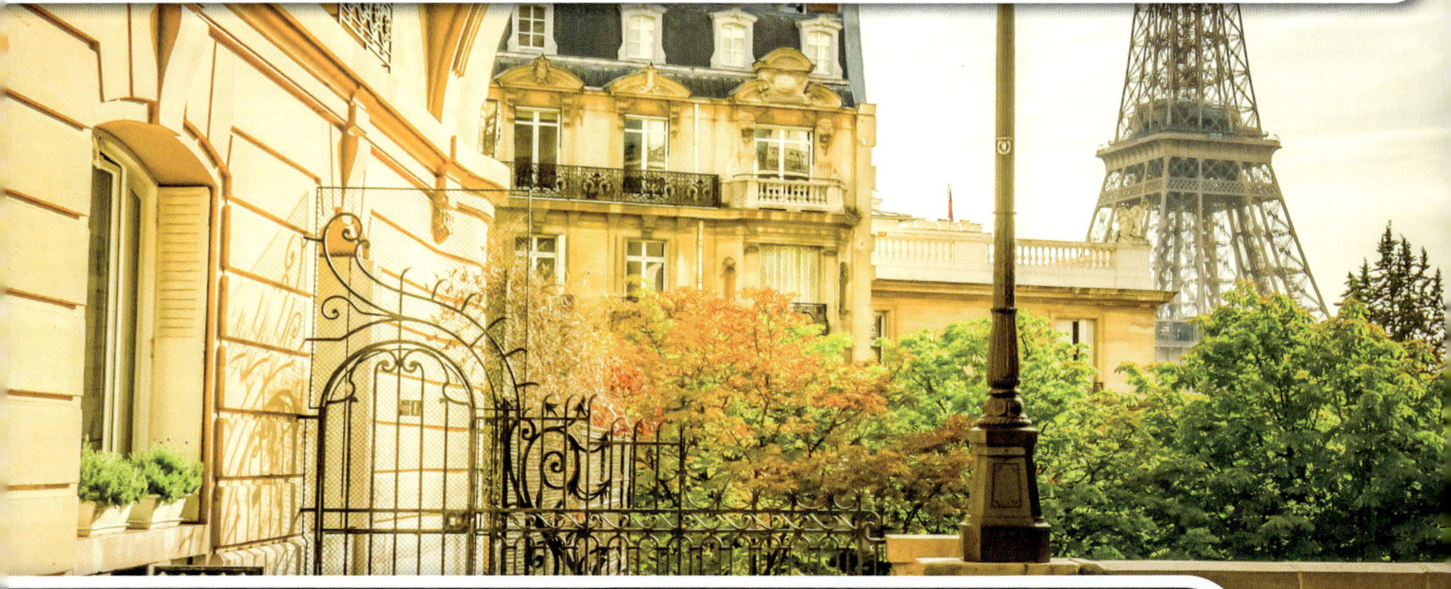

Image Credits

CONTENTS

Words that look like <u>this</u> can be found in the glossary on page 24.

WHERE IS FRANCE?

France is a country found on the continent of Europe. It is one of the biggest European countries.

The <u>official</u> language of France is French. Millions of people live in France's big cities, such as Paris and Marseille.

LANDSCAPE AND WEATHER

The weather in France changes with the seasons. It has warm summers and cool winters. The hottest months of the year are usually July and August.

The landscape in France changes from place to place. There are big cities, small farms, green forests, and high mountains.

RELIGION

There are many different <u>religions</u> that people follow. The religion with the most followers in France is Christianity. Most Christians in France are <u>Roman Catholic</u>.

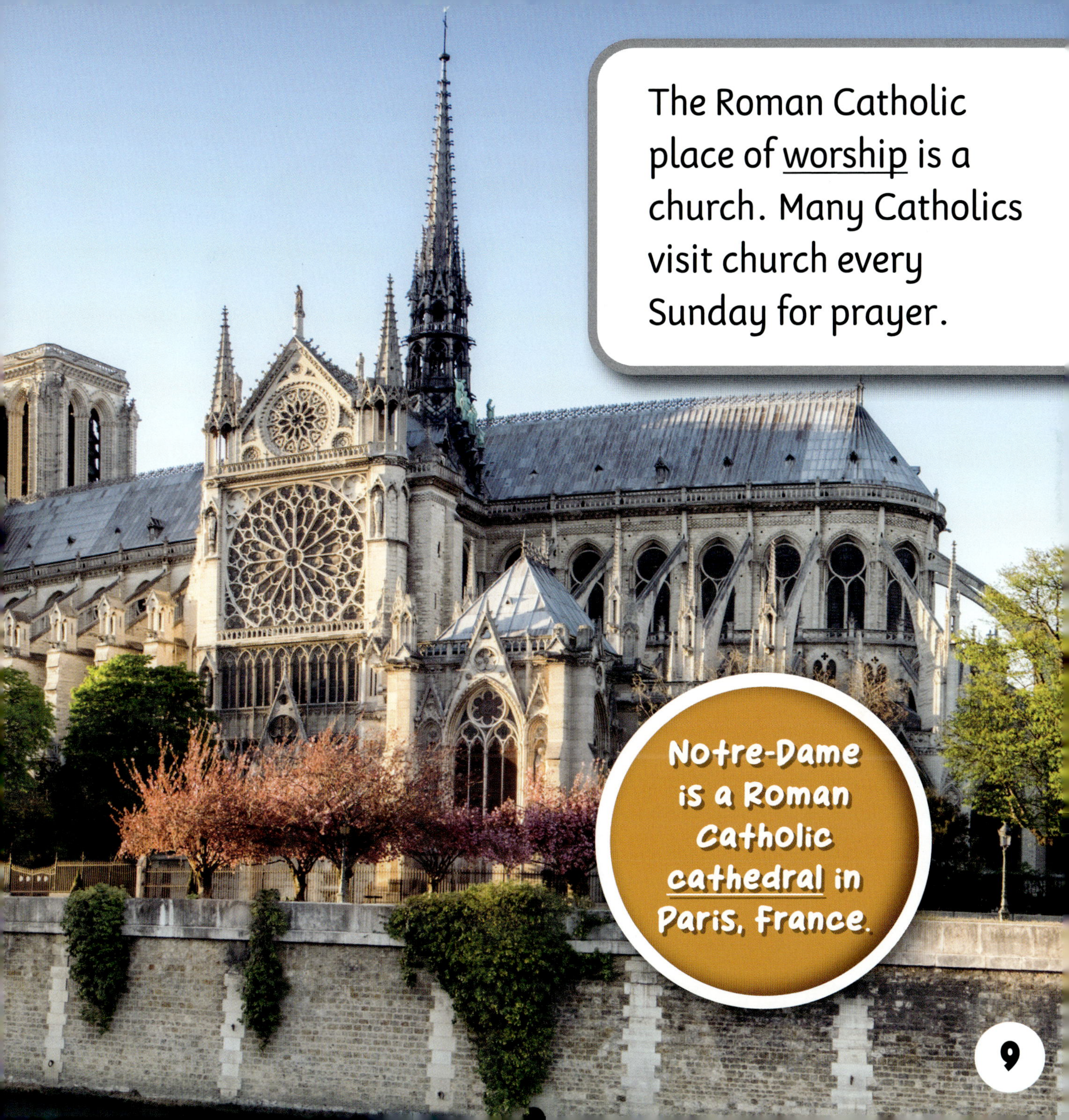

The Roman Catholic place of <u>worship</u> is a church. Many Catholics visit church every Sunday for prayer.

Notre-Dame is a Roman Catholic <u>cathedral</u> in Paris, France.

FAMILIES

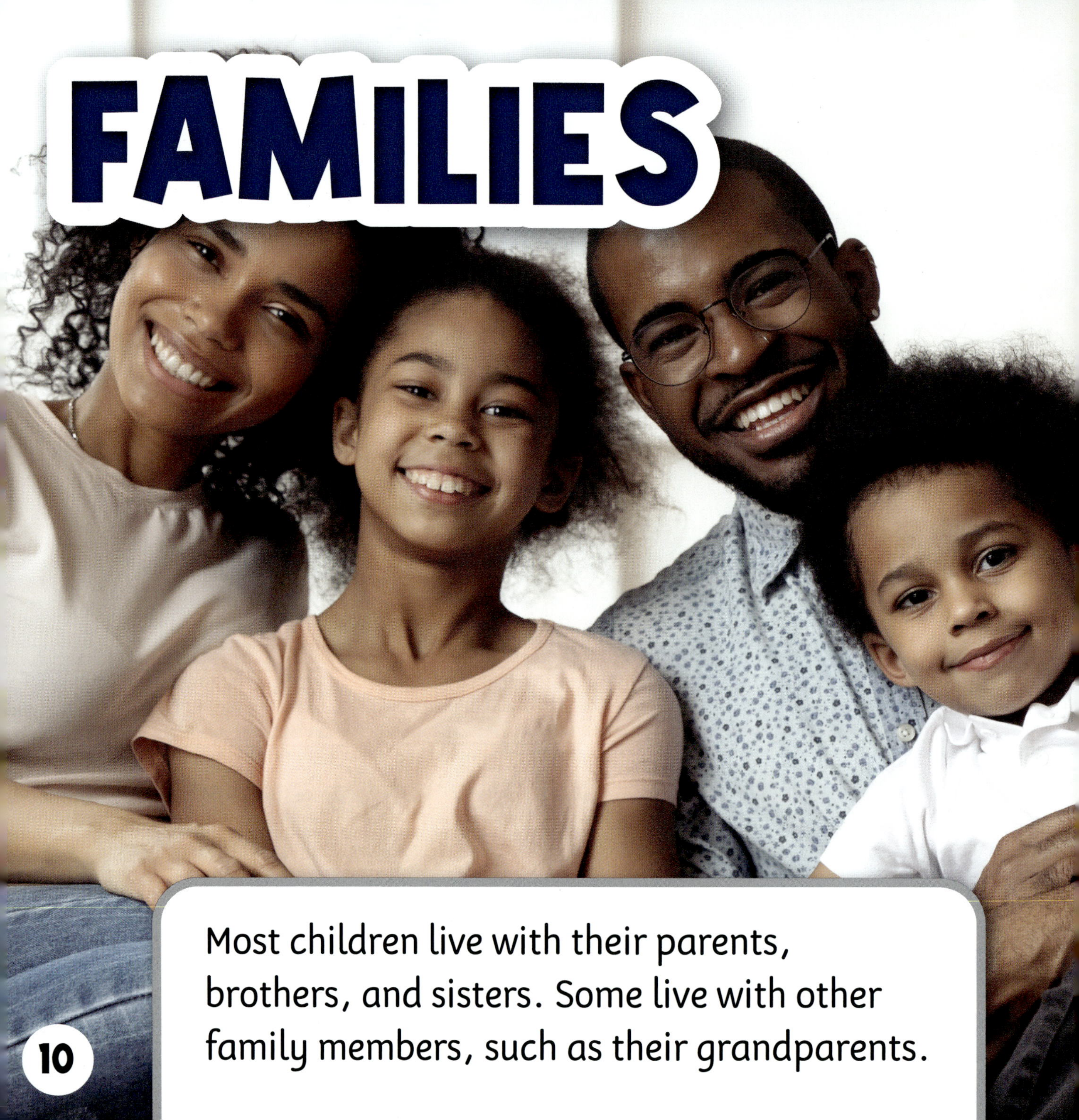

Most children live with their parents, brothers, and sisters. Some live with other family members, such as their grandparents.

In France, families often get together to celebrate Christian <u>holidays</u>, such as Christmas and Easter.

SCHOOL

In France, children start school at 3 years old and usually study until they are 18 years old. Some French primary schools are closed on Wednesdays.

Children in France study French, math, science, history, and another language, such as English. Most children go to school to study, but some children are taught at home.

HOME

Many people in France live in big cities. In cities, such as Paris, most of the people live in apartments. Some windows have wooden shutters to keep the rooms cool in the summers.

A lot of people also live in the countryside. Many farmers grow olive trees there. The olives can be eaten or made into oil for cooking.

CLOTHING

French people mostly wear <u>modern</u> clothing, such as jeans and T-shirts. The <u>traditional</u> French hat is called a beret.

For <u>festivals</u> and parties, people sometimes dress up in traditional French clothes. Women may wear white blouses, bonnets, and long skirts.

17

SPORTS

Sports such as basketball, tennis, soccer, and rugby are all very popular in France.

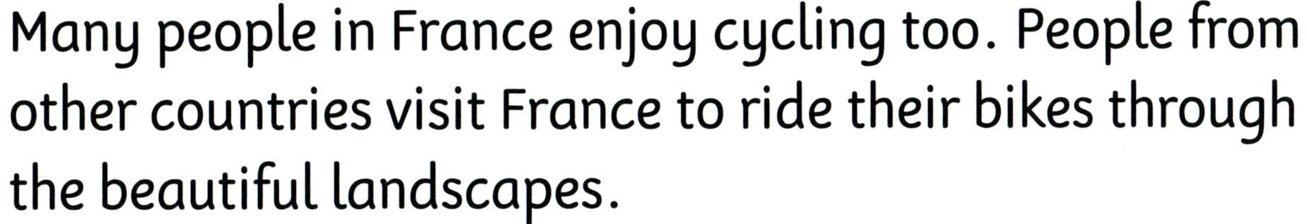

Many people in France enjoy cycling too. People from other countries visit France to ride their bikes through the beautiful landscapes.

France is home to the Tour de France, which is the world's most famous cycling race.

FOOD

France is known for making some of the best cheese, bread, and wine in the world. Loaves of bread called baguettes can be eaten with most meals.

There are many traditional French treats that are now eaten and enjoyed all around the world. Croissants and macarons are enjoyed in France and other countries.

21

FUN FACTS

Millions of people visit Paris every year. They visit the Louvre, the Eiffel Tower, Notre-Dame, and the Arc de Triomphe.

Mont Blanc is France's highest mountain, at over 15,750 feet (4,800 m). The Loire is France's longest river, at over 620 miles (1,000 km) long.

GLOSSARY

cathedral — a large building used for Christian worship

continent — a very large area of land that is usually made up of many countries

festivals — times when people come together to celebrate special events

modern — to do with recent or present times

official — to do with something that is recognized as having power or being important

religions — systems of faith and worship, especially to do with a god or gods

Roman Catholic — to do with the type of Christianity that follows the beliefs of the Roman Catholic Church

traditional — to do with beliefs, customs, or ways of behaving that have been around for a long time

vineyards — areas of land where grapes are grown

worship — religious acts of praise, such as prayer

INDEX